Com,

For Those
Who Grieve

Jeannie Ewing

Our Sunday Visitor

www.osv.com
Our Sunday Visitor Publishing Division
Our Sunday Visitor, Inc.
Huntington, Indiana 46750

Nihil Obstat
Msgr. Michael Heintz, Ph.D.
Censor Librorum

Imprimatur
✠ Kevin C. Rhoades
Bishop of Fort Wayne-South Bend
September 10, 2018

Copyright © 2018 by Our Sunday Visitor, Inc. Written by Jeannie Ewing. Published 2018.

23 22 21 20 19 18   1 2 3 4 5 6 7 8 9

Our Sunday Visitor Publishing Division, Our Sunday Visitor, Inc., 200 Noll Plaza, Huntington, IN 46750; 1-800-348-2440

ISBN: 978-1-68192-365-9 (Inventory No. T2205)
LCCN: 2018957809

Cover design: Tyler Ottinger
Cover art: Shutterstock
Interior design: Lindsey Riesen

PRINTED IN THE UNITED STATES OF AMERICA

INTRODUCTION

Devastating loss necessarily changes us. We move from a place of knowing to unknowing, certainty to uncertainty, joy to sorrow. Whatever the cause of your grief might be, your life has drastically changed. Before, life seemed hopeful, exuberant, and worthwhile. It was filled with light. Now the light has been extinguished. Suddenly, only darkness remains.

The contrast of light and darkness is a common spiritual metaphor found throughout Jewish and Christian tradition. Peek in your Bible, and you'll see several verses on the subject in both the Old and New Testaments. The light, which represents God, heals. Light warms our hearts when they have been chilled by grief, and it brings color back into our lives when darkness has left its shadow upon our souls.

Perhaps the light of hope and joy in your life faded weeks ago, or perhaps it has been decades.

Maybe you suffered sudden or lingering loss — of a spouse, a parent, a sibling. Maybe your loss was of a dream or deep desire in your heart. Perhaps you have lost a job or home, or you are experiencing financial strain or divorce. All of these things can be catalysts for the darkness of grief too.

No one wants to remain stuck in grief. We all long to be fully alive, to laugh again and relish treasured memories. Even if our memories are largely painful, we pray for healing and peace to replace the restlessness, anger, and fear that often accompany loss.

When you're hurting in the aftermath of loss, the last thing you can imagine doing is to journey with someone else who is suffering. And it's true that you must begin your own path of healing before attempting to help someone else bear their own wounds. At the same time, because of your experience of grief, you may become what Henri Nouwen called a "wounded healer." Our brokenness — our darkness — does not have to keep us from discovering a new way of life: one that is different than before we experienced loss, but still full of wonder.

Yes, right now you probably feel that darkness will never leave you, that you will always be separated from the joy of living. But your grief is an invitation to something more, something greater than your pain.

Often, the very event that creates the most suffering in our lives carries within it a call, a mission. You might not see it now. Anything that is good or beautiful or true may seem very far away, and that's okay. Be patient with yourself, but be open too. Allow yourself to be led by the Holy Spirit, who wants to set your heart ablaze with love once again. When you choose to love yourself and be available to others who are experiencing loss, you will discover the fire of divine charity within you. And through your own healing journey — which may take a lifetime — you will find that you can be a light to others along the way.

Author and editor Heidi Hess Saxton offered this reminder: "Don't forget to light your lamp. Don't forget to speak, to lend a hand when you can. Above all, don't forget what a kindness it can be to ask someone to leave his lamp burning, to give him confidence that he won't always be alone."[1]

Even if you feel shrouded in the darkness of grief, you *can* somehow still reflect God's Light. Even — especially — in the midst of great suffering, if only you remain faithful to the source of light, you can reflect that light to others. Allow God to fuel your lamp each day as you return to him in true devotion. And day after day, despite what you feel or experience, you will share that light with others. You will shine on his behalf without knowing how or when or why. You may only see your darkness, but others will see his light through you.

That's the invitation: in the midst of your sorrow, you can be a person of courage and faith. You don't have to feel "warm and fuzzy" to find light again. This devotional is designed to take your hand on your journey of grief, whether it is new and raw or aching and ongoing, and accompany you through the darkness and into the light of hope, healing, and wholeness.

---

1. Heidi Hess Saxton, *Lent with Saint Teresa of Calcutta: Daily Meditations* (Cincinnati, OH: Servant, 2017), pp. 12–13.

A Saint of Darkness

*If I ever become a saint, I will surely
be one of "darkness." I will continually be
absent from Heaven to light the light of those
in darkness on earth.*
Saint Teresa of Calcutta

Saint Teresa of Calcutta spent decades living in a hidden spiritual darkness. Others saw her outward, valiant generosity and kindness, but inwardly she experienced an intense void. For years, she felt no sign or consolation from God.

When you are hurting in the wake of devastating loss, you might feel the same way Mother Teresa did. You may cry out to God in desperation but receive no response to your prayer. Perhaps you are angry. It is normal and okay to feel angry, but in your anger you might build emotional barriers around your heart in an attempt to alleviate your pain. This might provide relief for a time, but in reality it only separates you all the more from receiving love and healing.

If only you could love like you did before your loss! Your pain is dark, because it reminds you of the light you once had or shared, which no longer exists. While you may be tempted to believe that it's better to protect yourself from ever feeling like this again, remember that love is always worth the risk. Mother Teresa's life is a shining example of this reality.

PRAYER

Heavenly Father, right now I am so lost in darkness. But I turn to you today, asking that you lift the darkness and reveal to me your never-ending light. I want to love again.

REFLECTION

What is most consoling to you about Saint Teresa's words, "I will light the light of those in darkness on earth"?

THE LIGHT OF A CANDLE

*All the darkness in the world cannot extinguish
the light of a single candle.*
ATTRIBUTED TO SAINT FRANCIS OF ASSISI

"Everything happens for a reason."
"She/he's in a better place now."
"We just have to accept God's plan."

For a thousand unhelpful words that ring hollow
in your heart, there is always at least one person
who says the very thing you need to hear: *"I can't
imagine what you're going through right now."
"You're right; this isn't fair. I'm here for you."*

You know people generally mean well when
they offer a common response to death or loss.
But it only adds to your darkness. That one person who isn't afraid to listen to your anguish and
who truly wants to accompany you through it
— that's the light of a single candle. Maybe you

haven't found that person yet. That's okay too. Let Jesus be that comforting presence in your life. He's ready and waiting.

Wherever the light comes from, that tiny flicker is enough to get you through today, to spark newfound hope in the depths of your soul, and to carry you to a place where you can see life as it truly is, in all its splendor and mystery.

PRAYER

"O most blessed Light divine, / shine within these hearts of yours, / and our inmost being fill!"[2]

REFLECTION

Think of one or two people who have given you real encouragement on your grief journey, then pray for them. If no one has, pray that God will provide that person for you.

---

2. From *Veni, Sancte Spiritus*.

DEEP AND HIDDEN THINGS

*"He reveals deep and hidden things /
and knows what is in the darkness, / for the light
dwells with him."*

DANIEL 2:22

If you've ever been snorkeling or deep-sea diving, you know that there are countless shades of ocean water. In shallow areas, the water is colorful, bluer than the deeper ends. If all you can see is a black hole under the ocean's surface, you know the water is very deep.

Darkness intimidates us, and perhaps with good reason. For instance, when deep-sea diving we know to avoid the dark water unless we have a lot of experience, as the depth can be dangerous for us. But when it comes to our spiritual lives, we don't have to be intimidated by things we cannot understand. God has revealed much about himself to us through Scripture and Sacred

Tradition, but he is still a vast mystery. There is depth to God that is beyond what we can possibly fathom, and that depth can seem scary.

But God is all light. What appears dark about him only seems that way to us because we can't see beyond the surface. In a similar way, try to remember that even the darkness in your grief carries within it some light. No matter what you see or how you feel, goodness is there.

Prayer
Jesus, help me see the light through your life when I am lost in the midst of my own darkness.

Reflection
What does it mean to you that God "reveals deep and hidden things" while you are suffering loss?

A Prayer of Trust

Psalm 34:1–7

I will bless the Lord at all times;
    his praise shall be always in my mouth.
My soul will glory in the Lord;
    let the poor hear and be glad.
Magnify the Lord with me;
    and let us exalt his name together.

I sought the Lord, and he answered me,
    delivered me from all my fears.
Look to him and be radiant,
    and your faces may not blush for shame.
This poor one cried out and the Lord heard,
    and from all his distress he saved him.

Scattered by Light

Darkness can only be scattered by light. Hatred can only be conquered by love.[3]
Pope Saint John Paul II

When we think of what operates in darkness, we usually imagine dirty creatures, like rats and cockroaches, which scatter when light is shone upon them. The darkness of grief tends to make our hearts feel dirty and ugly, too, because they have been wounded by an inexplicable pain.

But picture God shining his light upon your heart. He is sending forth his rays of light into your heart and soul, even though you can't necessarily see or feel it. Will you scatter, or will you turn your face upward to heaven and allow the light to transform you?

It's easy to allow our hearts to become hard-

---

3. Pope John Paul II, Address of His Holiness Pope John Paul II to the Diplomatic Corps (January 10, 2002), 7.

ened after we've experienced loss. Protecting ourselves from further heartbreak is an automatic defense against pain. Sometimes without realizing it, we put up protective barriers to God shining his light into our hearts, and while this seems to bring relief, it only extends our pain. But light brings clarity, and clarity leads us to being "conquered by love."

PRAYER
Lord, shatter the darkness of my pain today, and scatter your light through the holes left in my heart. Shine on me, that I may be conquered by your love.

REFLECTION
Where do you think God might be trying to scatter your darkness with his light?

THE LIGHT THAT ILLUMINATES THE DARKNESS

God is the light that illuminates the darkness,
even if it does not dissolve it, and a spark of
divine light is within each of us.[4]

POPE FRANCIS

If you've ever attended the Easter Vigil, you have experienced the striking contrast between candlelight and darkness. The soft, warm glow of a single candle suddenly multiplies, until more of what was once immersed in darkness becomes visible.

Yet the light of the candles does not eliminate the darkness completely; there are still pockets of it hiding in the corners or dancing in

---

4. Pope Francis, *God Is Always Near: Conversations with Pope Francis*, Giuseppe Costa, ed.; Gerard Seromik, trans. (Huntington, IN: Our Sunday Visitor, 2015), p. 124.

the shadows. Your grief is very similar. You have flickers and flashes of healing and hope — the light — when you receive a handwritten, heartfelt card, a homemade meal, or a thoughtful gift. But you still live in the midst of pockets of darkness sometimes.

Remember that there is always the spark of hope within you. The Holy Spirit illumines your suffering with his divine presence. He consoles, comforts, and heals your broken heart.

PRAYER
Holy Spirit, illuminate my mind, warm my heart, and renew the spark of hope in me today.

REFLECTION
Think of one activity that helps renew the spark of hope in your life when you are struggling. Then do it.

SEE GOD IN ALL THINGS

Faith is like a bright ray of sunlight. It enables us to see God in all things as well as all things in God.
SAINT FRANCIS DE SALES

Sometimes grief knocks gently but persistently on the door of our hearts, but there are other moments in life when loss strikes us suddenly and unexpectedly, like a dagger to the heart. Saint Francis de Sales knew this jarring kind of loss that drew him into a place of deep-seated sorrow when his younger sister, whom he baptized as an infant, died without warning at the age of fifteen.

Despite this loss, which Saint Francis described as his heart being broken in a way he could not have believed possible,[5] he maintained

---

5. Father Joseph M. Esper, "The Saints and Overcoming Grief," *Catholic Exchange* (October 29, 2015), https://catholicexchange.com /the-saints-and-overcoming-grief.

hope in the God he had come to know and love. Through the darkness of his grief, he was able to "see God in all things," even in suffering.

It's hard to imagine that faith can be a ray of sunlight when your life has been stricken with sorrow and incomprehensible loss. When grief is raw, it's as if your faith has been eclipsed by the night, and you cannot see the goodness in anything.

Perhaps today you can look for God everywhere and in everyone around you. That may be the key to finding the light of faith once again.

PRAYER

Lord God, I admit my faith is troubled during times of suffering and loss. Help me to find you in the people I meet and the places I go today.

REFLECTION

Think of one to two blessings or answered prayers from your past, meditating on how God was in all things and all things were in God. Then thank him in prayer.

LEAD US TO THE LIGHT

*When we feel temptations … we should run to
the side of our Mother in Heaven…. She will
defend us and lead us to the light.*

SAINT JOSEMARÍA ESCRIVÁ

Temptations come in many forms when you
grieve: anger directed at God, denial, blame,
cynicism, isolation. Your wounds and brokenness often travel with you for years, even decades, of your life. You might become hopeless
after a time, when nothing seems to be improv-
ing and everything is a struggle.

Who can aid you in the most difficult of
times? The Blessed Mother. You've probably
heard that she is the most powerful interces-
sor at your disposal, but have you really turned
to her in desperation and with confidence?
There's a very important difference between
developing a formal, distant devotion to her

and an authentic relationship with her as your mother.

Remember that she is Our Lady of Sorrows, and reflect on what pierced her heart. Many saints, including Saint Alphonsus Liguori, believed that Our Lady was given knowledge of her son's suffering when he was only a baby, perhaps during the prophecy of Simeon in the Temple at his presentation. From that point on, she grieved continuously, even as she rejoiced in the glory of raising the Son of God.

When you run to Our Lady, she will quickly and often miraculously lead you toward the light of her son.

PRAYER
Blessed Mother, be a mother to me now.

REFLECTION
What is the most desperate situation you're in right now? Give it wholeheartedly to Our Lady with confidence that she will help you.

IN LIGHT AND LOVE

*The Eucharist bathes the
tormented soul in light and love.*
SAINT BERNADETTE SOUBIROUS

If you compare grief to colors, you might say it is black or sometimes gray: everything dismal, dreary, and lackluster. The darkness of grief feels heavy and cumbersome. It torments you with the "what ifs" or "if onlys" that can never be answered this side of heaven. You live with regrets, questions, and mysteries.

Receiving Jesus in the Eucharist is an immense consolation when you are immersed in the black void of grief, even when you don't feel uplifted or instantly at peace. It's the grace of the Sacrament of Healing that penetrates your sorrow and bathes you in the vibrant colors of healing and joy.

The light is what you seek, even though it

seems so distant and unattainable when you are in pain. Run to the Eucharist and allow Jesus to consume you as you consume him. In time, his quiet presence will open your heart and bring light and love back into your life.

PRAYER
Jesus, I long for the comfort of your presence to fill my entire being. Consume me in the Sacrament of the Eucharist often.

REFLECTION
Recall one or two times in your life when the Eucharist has been a source of light and love when you were struggling. Thank Jesus by offering him a holy hour.

LIGHT THE ROAD

My Holy Guardian Angel, cover me with your
wing. With your fire light the road that I'm
taking. Come direct my steps ... help me. I call
upon you just for today.
SAINT THÉRÈSE OF LISIEUX

Most of us underestimate the power of our
guardian angel's presence and intercession in
our life. If you're like me, you probably learned
the "Angel of God" prayer as a child, and on oc-
casion — usually when something goes awry —
you imagine your angel watching over you or
protecting you from harm.

In reality, your guardian angel wants a relationship with you. He longs for you to pray
to him daily, to call on him when you get behind the wheel to drive, when you are making a
presentation at work, or when you are trying to
make a difficult decision. You can also invoke

other people's guardian angels. Pray to your children's angels when they leave for college; pray to a loved one's angel when that person is living a reckless lifestyle.

And when you grieve, is there another spiritual entity so close to you in your sorrow? Your guardian angel *chose* to love you, had full knowledge of every detail of your life before you were born, and is your most faithful friend in time of need. Call upon your angel just for today, and he will not fail you.

PRAYER

Dear guardian angel, thank you for always protecting me, guiding my steps, and lighting the way when I feel lost, alone, or afraid.

REFLECTION

When have you recognized your guardian angel at work in your life, especially when you were struggling?

LIGHT HAS ARISEN

"… the people who sit in darkness / have seen a great light, / on those dwelling in a land overshadowed by death / light has arisen."

MATTHEW 4:16

Life isn't always black and white, and grief reminds us of this striking reality. When you are grieving, truths and life lessons you may have accepted before your loss suddenly become murky. You may begin to question everything — including your faith.

It's perfectly normal to ask God "Why?" following a devastating loss. Everything, both good and bad, must pass through his hands before happening. And that can be the hardest reality of all to accept: that God already knew you would experience this specific suffering before it happened. Why, then, did he allow it? It seems so cruel.

When grief overshadows your life, you can turn to Scripture for the reminder of who God is — always loving, faithful, kind, and merciful. Likewise, Scripture (especially the psalms) can encourage you when you are overshadowed by darkness.

As Christians, we cannot remain stuck in the thick of our pain. Instead, we look to the great light of hope that lies beyond what we can see or even imagine right now.

PRAYER

Lord, I know you are always good and kind, but right now I feel so lost and alone. Help me to see the light of hope in the midst of my darkness.

REFLECTION

Meditate on the meaning of light in your life. Reflect on its material properties, spiritual qualities, and the benefits you gain from light.

GOD, THE LOOKING GLASS

The accidents of life separate us from our dearest friends, but let us not despair. God is like a looking glass in which souls see each other. The more we are united to him by love, the nearer we are to those who belong to him.
SAINT ELIZABETH ANN SETON

If you've ever heard of Saint Elizabeth Ann Seton, it's likely you don't consider her the patron saint of grief. She is most renowned for her establishment of the first Catholic schools (and the school system as we know it) in the United States and for founding a religious order, the Sisters of Charity, whose primary apostolate was to help the poor.

But Saint Elizabeth was no stranger to loss. Born to a wealthy Anglican family, she eventually lost her social status and money after her conversion to Catholicism. Many of her friends shut her out of their lives, too, because they didn't agree with her religious preference.

Though she was privileged to enjoy a happy and fruitful marriage to William Seton, he and two of their five children died, one after the other, in a short period of time. Her emotional languishing did not deter her strong faith in God. She clung to him in the belief that her love and fidelity to God would draw her closer to the ones she lost.

In your journey of grief, consider how you might draw closer to the people you have lost to death or estrangement. Imagine that God is the "looking glass" that reflects his love upon your heart, and through which you can remain spiritually close to your loved ones who have passed into eternal life.

PRAYER

Heavenly Father, I want to see once again the ones I've loved and lost. I know I can be near to them through you. Grant me a portion of your love today, that I may reflect your love to those who remain with me on earth.

REFLECTION

Write a letter to God or a beloved person you've lost through death or separation. You don't have to mail it. Just allow it to be the means by which you draw closer to them in love.

DO NOT DESPAIR

*"O soul steeped in darkness, do not despair.
All is not yet lost. Come and confide in your
God, who is love and mercy."*
JESUS TO SAINT FAUSTINA

If you haven't already, you may have moments in
your grief journey when you are enraged at God,
questioning his motives, wondering how he
could do something so cruel. Your pain reminds
you of this apparent punishment, and you feel as
if your soul is immersed in despair.

During these times, cling to hope. Even if it
is the smallest of threads or the tiniest flicker of
a flame, hope is your light. It reminds you of the
little resurrections happening all around you today and of the greatest Resurrection of all. Hope
helps you to accept the mysteries and questions
of life without needing all the answers.

Hope leads to meekness, which softens the

heart in the midst of pain. An open heart is a re-
ceptive one, capable of receiving God's abundant
mercy and grace. Hold fast to hope and pour
your miseries into the Heart of Jesus. There you
will receive healing and peace as you surrender
your questions and anger.

PRAYER

Sacred Heart of Jesus, hide me in your wounds,
that by your stripes I may be healed.

REFLECTION

How can you find the little resurrections today
that will lead you closer to hope and away from
the darkness of despair?

A Spark of Light

Every believer must be a spark of light,
a center of love.
POPE SAINT JOHN XXIII

A few years ago, I read a jarring statement: "Everyone you meet is fighting a battle you know nothing about. Be kinder than necessary." It seems that everywhere you go in public, people are gloomy, weighed down by their invisible burdens. Few people smile, make eye contact, or even exhibit common courtesy.

It's easy to allow the burdens of others to weigh you down. But if you remember to be a spark of light and center of love in the world, you can encounter others in their suffering by offering a cheerful hello, a warm smile, and a sincere compliment.

My middle daughter, Sarah, is a natural at this. She has a rare disease, so we are in medical facilities on a regular basis. Those who are in the waiting rooms with us are clearly dealing with heavy issues. But Sarah greets everyone personally. She smiles, waves, asks people their names — and it's as if the weight of the world is instantly lifted from their shoulders.

Sometimes being that spark of light to others can ease our pain too. Since Sarah's birth, I have met countless parents of kids who have various disabilities, and we share our bittersweet journeys. Through my writing about my experience of suffering, I have received encouragement from countless readers. Doing something positive with my pain to accompany those who are struggling thus often lessens my own pain.

PRAYER

Heavenly Father, help me to bring light to someone suffering today.

REFLECTION

Notice people you encounter today who seem to be struggling. Choose to be kinder than necessary.

A Bright Ray of Sun

Start being brave about everything. Drive out
darkness and spread light. Don't look at your
weaknesses. Realize instead that in Christ
crucified you can do everything.
SAINT CATHERINE OF SIENA

Life as a caregiver can be daunting and over-
whelming. Chronic grief settles in my daily
routine, and I easily become discouraged by the
minutiae of each struggle. Even on summer days
when the sun's heat and light are beating on my
skin, I can only see what's not there at the mo-
ment: the lack of fun and freedom, and the loneliness of this journey.

During these times in your own life, it's im-
possible to rely on your emotions to guide you
through suffering and sorrow. Emotions are
fickle and fragile. Yet the reality of life, despite
what you may feel today, is that God is always

good and always loving. Faith is more than a feeling, and you can choose faith and cling to it even when your feelings are very dark.

God's unfailing goodness must be the reason for your fidelity during really trying times. Truth alone reveals that God is everywhere and in all things, so that you, too, can say with the saints, "All is well" and "Everything is grace."

PRAYER

Holy Spirit, strengthen in me the virtue of faith, especially as my spirits sink and doubts assail me.

REFLECTION

Where can you find and appreciate the pockets of sunshine in your life today?

My Life and My Light

Stay with me, Lord, for you are my light, and without you I am in darkness.

SAINT PIO OF PIETRELCINA

There are two different kinds of darkness that can afflict you when you are in the throes of grief: unholy and holy darkness.

Unholy darkness is the result of sin — maybe your own or someone else's — and affects all of creation with disease, burdens, problems, and death. Unholy darkness is what draws you away from God and into the pit of discouragement, depression, despondency, and despair.

Holy darkness, however, is a kind of *hidden* light. There are times when you suffer and believe God has abandoned you. You cannot see him. You don't feel his presence. When you pray, you don't hear his voice. You receive no consolations or signs like you may have during sweeter times. Penetrating loneliness settles upon your soul, and you can't shake the feeling that God isn't there and doesn't care.

If you are faithful to God during these times of spiritual desolation, and you are frequenting the sacraments of Penance and the Eucharist, you may be experiencing holy darkness. There are times when God wants us to love him for his sake, rather than for what he does for us. Like the beloved line in the poem "Footprints," you can trust that during these times, he is carrying you.

Prayer
Lord God, I feel so alone right now. Be with me, strengthen me, and help me to keep moving forward in faith.

Reflection
Think of one or two tangible ways you can increase your fidelity and devotion to God this week.

My Light and
My Salvation

The Lord is my light and my salvation; /
whom should I fear? / The Lord is my life's refuge; /
of whom should I be afraid?

Psalm 27:1

Grief can plunge you into all sorts of uncomfortable and ugly emotions: shame, guilt, anger, depression, and fear. Fear may be the blanket emotion for many feelings you are experiencing, and it always leads you into a place of spiritual darkness. When you combat fear, however, you grow in courage and thus are strengthened in the theological virtues of faith, hope, and charity.

We do not need to fear death, because as Christians we know it's not the end. Grief reminds us, even through our deepest fears, that life is transitory. Change is hard. But we can manage every significant change with a perspective of salvation.

What can be saved or salvaged when you are hurting and sorrowful? For me, it's the smallest moments of grace: the cardinal singing outside my kitchen window; a lone rose blooming among weeds; a clear blue sky and soft, gentle breeze; a smile and hug from one of my children; an unexpected note or visit from a friend.

Look for the light, and remember there is always something redeemable in the ashes of your life.

Prayer

Lord, I am afraid of death, suffering, and my own pain. Help me to see your movements of grace in my life today.

Reflection

Write down one or two of your deepest fears and ways you can find courage to overcome them.

THE LIGHT SHINING
IN THE DARKNESS

*... the light shines in the darkness, / and the
darkness has not overcome it.*

JOHN 1:5

Sometimes grief consumes you. It feels suffo-
cating and heavy. It's the worst invisible burden,
because it's known only to you and God. There's
no way to escape from yourself, so grief can trap
you in a spiral of negative thinking. It can para-
lyze you into inaction or apathy.

John spoke truth to this kind of suffering.
He wrote that darkness cannot consume us, because the light of Jesus ultimately breaks through
the darkness. Consider the cycles of night and
day: even at night we have the moon's soft glow
and the bright illumination of stars and planets.
We are never completely cloaked in darkness;
there's always a source of light if we look for it.

Much of the hard work in your grief journey pertains to your worldview. It becomes temporarily skewed when you suffer grave losses — you can only see trials and troubles. You often overlook anything good, however small it may be.

Today, look for the light, even if it's the smallest twinkling star in the blackest of your nights.

Prayer

Heavenly Father, I forget about the greatness of your love for me when I'm hurting. Show me the goodness in my life today.

Reflection

Take a brief walk today in nature and notice the gifts of God's goodness all around you. Thank him for blessing your life.

PRAYER

The Light of Hope
by Jeannie Ewing

Lord, teach me to pray
Even when I am in the throes of darkness
And cannot see the beauty of sunshine or
Feel the warmth of your love.

Lord, help me walk with you
When the path is strewn with thorns and rocks
And grief blackens my heart.
I want to carry the light of hope
In my heart as I journey toward heaven.

Lord, guide me to love
When I am suffering, sick, or sorrowful,
For I know that you will turn all crosses into
    victories
And lead me from night to day. Amen.

THE LIGHT OF LIFE

Jesus spoke to them again, saying, "I am the light
of the world. Whoever follows me will not walk
in darkness, but will have the light of life."

JOHN 8:12

After my daughter Sarah was born, I didn't want
to follow Jesus to the cross. Her birth revealed
a lot of things about myself I never knew: that I
wanted to choose my own path of redemption;
that I was selfish and only wanted an easy, comfortable life; and that following Jesus, for me,
meant doing things my way and on my time.

In a short period of time, I had to confront
the fact that life wouldn't be comfortable or easy
anymore. In fact, it would be entirely unpredict-
able and possibly chaotic. Do you ever feel that
way when your world is flipped upside down,
backward, and shaken to the core?

Grief can jolt you in many ways. You often

see a side of yourself that seems ugly, and you'd rather hide from yourself. But Jesus wants you to walk in truth, and the only way to live as a son or daughter of the Light is to face your pain and walk through it, day by day.

PRAYER
Jesus, grant me the courage to follow wherever you lead me.

REFLECTION
Meditate on what it means to "take up your cross daily" and follow Jesus. Imagine walking with him from Gethsemane to Golgotha.

CROOKED WAYS STRAIGHT

*I will lead the blind on a way they do not know;
/ by paths they do not know I will guide them.
/ I will turn darkness into light before them, /
and make crooked ways straight. / These are my
promises: / I made them, I will not forsake them.*

ISAIAH 42:16

When tragedy strikes, it makes us feel blind-sided. The tragedy might be a slow, expected death, or it can be a sudden accident. Grief is a crooked road, riddled with thorns and thickets. It's never the path you would choose; you are often thrust into it without warning. Grief doesn't ask your permission before it afflicts your life.

What, then, can heal as you traverse such a worn road? You're too weary to see anything ahead. In fact, all appears dismal as you put one foot in front of the other. How do you know if where you're going is leading you out of this hellish place of pain?

God's promises *never* fail. Even if you aren't sure where you're going, as long as you're moving forward, one step at a time, be assured that he is guiding you. One day, when you least expect it, you will discover the beauty of peace and contentment.

PRAYER

Lord God, I don't know where you're leading me, but I long to trust you. Help me to keep moving forward.

REFLECTION

Think back on another hard time in your life. What helped you get through it? How can you see more clearly today where God was leading you then?

Your Light Must Shine

"You are the light of the world. A city set on a mountain cannot be hidden. Nor do they light a lamp and then put it under a bushel basket; it is set on a lampstand, where it gives light to all in the house. Just so, your light must shine before others, that they may see your good deeds and glorify your heavenly Father."

MATTHEW 5:14–16

Your grief work is never complete until you pass on the wisdom you've gained to others who are in the throes of mourning. Your suffering has a greater purpose than you may realize at this point in your journey. Think of everyday heroes and heroines who stepped up to set their lights on a lampstand for others to benefit from what they learned.

I knew a family who lost a child when he was under eighteen months old. He had been in the care of a babysitter, who had a criminal history of child abuse they didn't know about, and he died due to her negligence. Even as they suffered, they spearheaded the implementation of statewide legislation making it mandatory for all day-care providers to disclose their criminal history to potential clients. They wanted to save other children from the same fate.

It's likely the good that comes from your own suffering will not be something straightforward or what you would want. But if you allow God's grace to unfurl in your heart, you will discover ways, both great and small, that you can make a difference in someone else's journey. Maybe you're the soothing balm to their festering wounds. Maybe you are the rock upon which they can lean.

Be open to where God is leading you.

Prayer
Jesus, help me to have the courage to reflect your light to others, rather than hiding behind my pain.

REFLECTION

Can you see possible ways God might be calling you to accompany others in their suffering? Make a list, pray about it, and consult with a trusted spiritual adviser. Then, begin.

About the Author

JEANNIE EWING believes the world ignores and rejects the value of the cross. As a Catholic spirituality author, she writes about the hidden value of suffering. Her books include a meditation journal, two devotionals, and two books on the topic of discovering joy in the midst of grief and waiting with expectation. She is a frequent guest on Catholic radio and contributes to several online and print Catholic periodicals. Jeannie lives in northern Indiana with her four children and husband, Ben. For more information about her books or to schedule a speaking engagement, please visit her website at http://jeannieewing.com. Follow Jeannie on social media at jeannie.ewing.author on Facebook and jeannieewing on Instagram.